D0906535

ON THE HUNT WITH
GREAT WHITE SHARKS

BY KRISTEN POPE

The Child's World®
childsworld.com

Published by The Child's World®
1980 Lookout Drive • Mankato, MN 56003-1705
800-599-READ • www.childsworld.com

Acknowledgments
The Child's World®: Mary Berendes, Publishing Director
Red Line Editorial: Design, editorial direction, and production
Photographs ©: Tim Davis/Corbis, cover, 1; Arend van der Walt/Shutterstock
Images, 4; Steven Allan/iStockphoto, 6; Sergey Uryadnikov/Shutterstock
Images, 8; Alexius Sutandio/Shutterstock Images, 9; Sylwia Domaradzka/
iStockphoto, 11; iStockphoto, 12, 15; Red Line Editorial, 14; Derek Heasley/
Shutterstock Images, 17; Emmanuel R. Lacoste/Shutterstock Images, 18;
Gerold Uder/iStockphoto, 21

ISBN 9781634074513

LCCN 2015946265

Printed in the United States of America
Mankato, MN
December, 2015
PA02279

TABLE OF CONTENTS

Chapter 1

ON THE HUNT

A great white shark slices through the ocean waters off the coast of California. It is on an early morning hunt. The smell of fresh blood fills its nostrils. A wounded animal is nearby. The blood could be up to 3 miles (4.8 km) away. Maybe it is the blood of a seal. Or a sea lion. Either one would make a tasty meal. Maybe the great white will be lucky enough to find a small, hurt whale.

Early morning is the best time for great whites to hunt. The shadows and dim light of early morning give the shark an advantage. Great white sharks sneak up on **prey** from below. It is hard for their prey to see the powerful **predator** lurking below. The topside, or **dorsal** side, of the shark is a slate gray color. It blends in well with the dark, rocky ocean floor. As for the great white's name, that comes from the shark's belly. It is the only part of the shark that is white.

The shark follows the scent. It could be just a tiny drop of blood. Or it could be much more. The only way to find out is to

◀ **A great white shark's dorsal fin cuts through the water as it swims near the surface.**

locate the bleeding animal. As the shark swims, it swims deeper and deeper in the water.

The blood is closer now. The shark's pitch black eyes dart around. It uses its eyes to hunt prey. Up above, it sees a seal. The seal is floating near the surface. It has a small gash on its side. This is the blood the shark smells.

Quietly, the shark swims closer. The wounded seal is not moving. Blood trickles into the water. The stronger smell of blood is making the shark even hungrier. The shark stays low on the ocean floor. As it gets closer, it starts to rise. Then it is time for the kill. In a flash, it races for the seal. The shark smashes its cone-shaped nose up into the seal. At the same time, the shark rips off a chunk of the seal. The shark's taste buds in its mouth and throat tell it the prey is a seal.

The seal thrashes. It tries to swim away. But there is no place to go. It is wounded and trapped. As the shark and seal battle, the shark's **ear stone** helps the shark know which way is up in the water. This helps it stay focused on the hunt.

Soon, the seal stops moving. More blood pours into the water. The shark opens its mouth. Its 300 teeth show. They are lined up in seven rows. With its **serrated** teeth, the shark rips off

◄ **Great white sharks hunt near the coast for seals and sea lions.**

▲ Great white sharks have cone-shaped
noses and dark black eyes.

another chunk of the seal. During the fight, the shark loses two of
its teeth. They swirl down and land on the ocean floor. It's okay,
though. New teeth will grow in their place. And the other 298
teeth serve just as well. Even with hundreds of teeth, the shark
doesn't use them for chewing. Using its narrower bottom teeth,
the shark holds the seal. Its larger upper teeth rip into the prey.
It tears hunks of flesh off. After ripping off each piece, the shark
swallows it whole.

◄ Some sea lions are quick enough to escape.

The shark's nose rises above the water. Its nose is scarred. Seals and sea lions fight when sharks try to eat them. Their claws and teeth can rip into the shark. Sometimes, this leaves scars. But the shark's latest battle with the seal doesn't leave any new scars. The shark rips off a few more hunks of seal. It gulps each one down. The seal is almost gone. After swallowing the last bit, the shark swims away. The sun is getting higher in the sky. Prime hunting time is over for now.

Jagged, triangular teeth line great white sharks' mouths. ▶

Chapter 2

LIFE UNDERWATER

The shark swims on as the sun rises higher. It is a **carnivore**. It hunts seals and sea lions. Those always make good meals. But its favorite prey is elephant seals. It is February, and it is the perfect time to find elephant seals. Each year from October to March, elephant seals swim in California's coastal waters.

But great whites don't just live off the coast in California. They live around the world. They are most commonly found in oceans near Australia, New Zealand, the United States, and South Africa. They only live in salt water. They can live in cold water or subtropical water.

The waters off the California coast are cold. This shark keeps on swimming in the chilly water. But that doesn't bother it. The shark is warm blooded. This means it can keep parts of its body warmer than the cool water around it.

◀ **Great white sharks are always looking for food.**

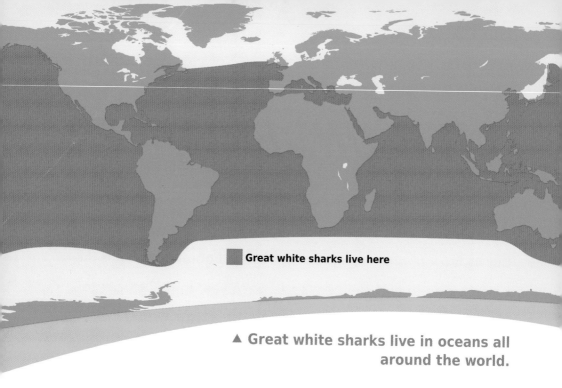

Great white sharks live here

▲ Great white sharks live in oceans all around the world.

Great whites can swim for very long distances. Stretching 18 feet (5 m) from the tip of its tail to its nose, it is massive. The great white is the largest predatory fish on the planet. Their large bodies make them master swimmers. Their torpedo-like shapes help them move through the water easily. And their massive tails are very powerful. When a great white sees something to eat, it can swim very fast. It can even **breach** out of the water to grab a meal.

The shark passes some plants underwater. It moves its 3,500 pounds (1,588 kg) through the water easily. Most sharks move their bodies back and forth while swimming. But the great white doesn't. It swims with a stiff body and moves its tail from side to side. As it swims, the shark's nostrils below its nose are visible.

Great white sharks have the greatest sense of smell of any kind of shark.

Suddenly, the shark senses a small fish swim by. Great whites can feel even the tiniest movements in the water. They can feel them from more than 820 feet (250 m) away. They can even tell in what direction prey is moving. The fish swims away. The

▲ Racing up to 35 miles (56 km) per hour, great white sharks breach to try and catch prey.

movements tell the shark it is just a small fish. It decides to let this one go. After all, it can't go after every fish in the ocean.

Farther ahead, the shark feels an electrical current from an animal. Nerves in animals make tiny magnetic fields. Most animals cannot feel these. But a great white shark can. It has special cells on its nose. These cells feel electrical currents. The cells can tell how strong an animal is and where it is. This special ability helps the shark hunt. It also helps it find its way across huge oceans. It can follow the magnetic map of the Earth to get where it is going. But today, it is just on the lookout for a good, large meal.

Soon, another great white appears. The two sharks will hunt together today. Later, one of the sharks kills a huge seal. Two other great whites smell the blood. They join the hunting party. All four sharks share the seal. This is normal for them when they hunt together. Sometimes they hunt alone. But great white sharks are social animals. They often swim and hunt together.

Sometimes great white sharks will share ▶
their catch with other sharks.

Chapter 3

NEW LIFE

The group of sharks swims out to sea. They pass a huge ship. A massive fishing net sits in the water. The sharks are all very careful to avoid the net. The nets are dangerous to sharks. Sharks can easily get tangled up in nets. If they are caught in a net, they could die. Sometimes humans hunt sharks for their teeth. Or they hunt sharks as trophies. Other people want to make shark fins into soup. Sharks are careful around humans. The group of sharks swims away. It will have to look for its next meal elsewhere.

One of the sharks in the group is a female. She is about to give birth. Her eggs grow and develop in her body. They will also hatch inside the mother's body. First, one 5-foot (1.5-m) long great white shark baby comes out of her. It is called a pup. Five more pups are born. They are all between 3 feet (0.9 m) and 5 feet (1.5 m) long. Sometimes, a great white shark mother will have up to 10 pups at a time. The great white shark pups quickly swim away. They do not stay with their mother. They are all on their own now.

◄ **Great white sharks are sometimes hunted and caught by humans.**

The newborn pups swim in different directions. They already know how to hunt. They swim and look for squid, stingrays, and even other small sharks. These all make good meals.

Scientists are not sure exactly where great white sharks are born. They think some may be born in southern California because the waters are warm. They think the sharks may swim north, into cooler waters, as they get bigger. Great white sharks can live to be more than 60 years old. In 10 years, the males will be ready to reproduce. Females can have their first pups when they are between 12 and 18 years old. By then, they will also be top predators.

Newborn pups hunt squid. ▶

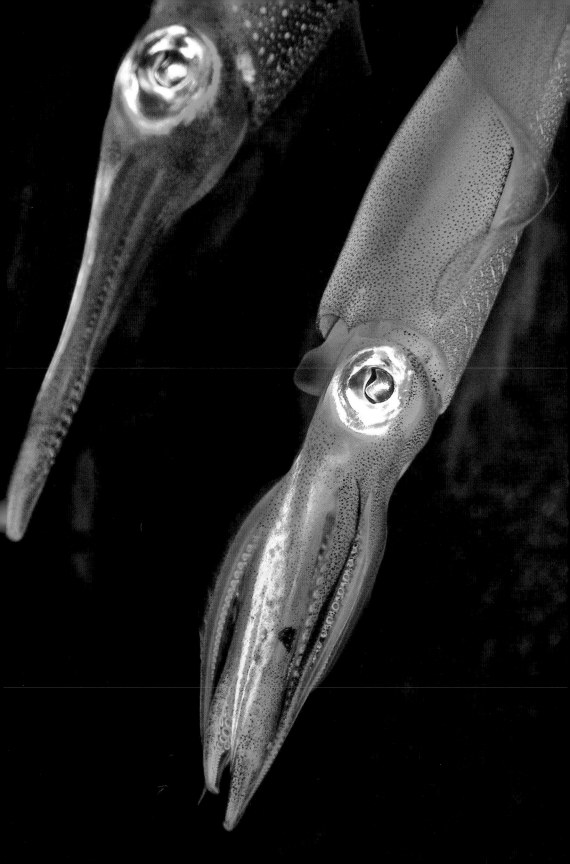

GLOSSARY

breach (breech): To breach means to break through something. Great white sharks sometimes breach the water when chasing a seal.

carnivore (KAHR-nuh-vor): A carnivore is an animal that eats meat. The great white shark is a carnivore.

dorsal (DOR-suhl): Something that is dorsal is on the top or back of an animal. The dorsal side and dorsal fin of the great white shark are a slate gray color.

ear stone (eer stone): An ear stone is part of an animal's ear that lets it know which way is up in the water. The great white shark's ear stone helps it swim and hunt.

predator (PRED-uh-ter): A predator is an animal that eats other animals. The great white shark is a top predator.

prey (PRAY): Prey are animals that are eaten by other animals. Seals and sea lions are great white sharks' prey.

serrated (SER-ay-tid): Something that is serrated has a jagged edge. The great white shark's teeth are serrated, helping it rip apart prey.

TO LEARN MORE

Books

Green, Jen. *Great White Shark*. New York: Bearport Publishing, 2014.

Loh-Hagan, Virginia. *Discover Great White Sharks*. Ann Arbor, MI: Cherry Lake Publishing, 2016.

Markovics, Joyce L. *Great White Shark*. New York: Bearport Publishing, 2016.

Web Sites

Visit our Web site for links about great white sharks:

childsworld.com/links

Note to Parents, Teachers, and Librarians: We routinely verify our Web links to make sure they are safe and active sites. So encourage your readers to check them out!

SELECTED BIBLIOGRAPHY

"Great White Shark." *Ocean Portal*. Smithsonian Institution, 2013. Web. 5 June 2015.

"Great White Shark." *WWF*. World Wildlife Fund, 2015. Web. 10 June 2015.

Raffaele, Paul. "Forget Jaws, Now it's . . . Brains!" *Smithsonian Magazine*. Smithsonian, 2008. Web. 4 June 2015.

INDEX

ABOUT THE AUTHOR

Kristen Pope is a writer and editor with years of experience working in national and state parks and museums. She has a master's degree in natural resources and has taught people of all ages about science and the environment. She has even coaxed reluctant insect-lovers to pet Madagascar hissing cockroaches.